**DATE DUE**     MAR 0 3

| | | | |
|---|---|---|---|
| | | | |
| | | | |
| | | | |
| | | | |
| | | | |
| | | | |
| | | | |
| | | | |
| | | | |
| | | | |
| | | | |
| | | | |
| | | | |
| | | | |
| | | | |
| | | | |
| | | | |
| | | | |
| GAYLORD | | | PRINTED IN U.S.A. |

MANZANITA TREE, CHANNEL ISLANDS, CALIFORNIA

LITTLE SUR RIVER, BIG SUR, CALIFORNIA

(BELOW) BEACH GRASS, GOLD BEACH, OREGON

(PAGE 7) SEA FIG DETAIL, BODEGA BAY, CALIFORNIA

(PAGE 8) BY-THE-WIND SAILORS, A KIND OF JELLYFISH,
POINT REYES NATIONAL SEASHORE, CALIFORNIA

(PAGE 9) MUSSELS AND SEAWEED, TATOOSH ISLAND, WASHINGTON

*This book is dedicated to my mother, Imogene, who showed me the wonder of God's world; and to my wife, Eva, who has imbued my life with love.*

*Tim Thompson*

Published by Thomasson-Grant, Inc.:
Frank L. Thomasson III and John F. Grant, Directors;
C. Douglas Elliott, Product Development;
Megan R. Youngquist, Art Director;
Jim Gibson, Production Manager;
Carolyn M. Clark, Senior Editor.
Designed by Carolyn Weary
Edited by Rebecca Beall Barns
Introduction by Wesley Marx

# THOMASSON-GRANT

# PACIFIC COAST
## A RUGGED HARMONY

PHOTOGRAPHY BY TIM THOMPSON

INTRODUCTION BY WESLEY MARX

A little child stands a bit unsteadily on the soft, sandy beach. He squats down, picks up one surf-polished pebble after another, and lets fly in the general direction of the world's largest ocean. When he finally scores a splashy direct hit, his shriek of joy merges with the cries of gulls overhead and the hiss of trapped air escaping from the swash of surf.

I suspect that's how my relationship with the Pacific shore began. I think of the discoveries that lay ahead for this new slinger of pebbles; days would come when I'd be knocked down by comber after comber until at last, for fleeting seconds, I could ride a wave to shore. I would venture into the surf with a face mask and learn that the flea-ridden kelp on the beach unravels into swaying forests offshore. I would walk through quiet, shaded redwood groves, then into the bright light of the open shore. At low tide I would dig barehanded for a pailful of butter clams as the sun set on the Pacific. There would be times spent by driftwood fires that kicked sparks into the night, lulling me to sleep with tomorrow's waves already cresting inside my head.

The shore can give a lifetime of experiences — sometimes when you least expect them. Once, while pulling on a wet suit for a dive into the kelp forests, I looked up to see a gray whale breach and fall back in a resplendent white splash. One day while cooling off in the Trinity River in northern California, I saw a salmon leap out of my swimming hole to clear a ledge. After evading nets, seals, coastal trollers, and bears, the salmon was headed upriver to spawn and die.

This shore will introduce you to the fog-shrouded redwoods, the tallest of trees, and the twisted elfin forests of chaparral, the dominant vegetation on the coastal slopes of southern California. The world's largest marine snail, the iridescent-shelled abalone, lives here as well as the world's largest burrowing clam, the homely geoduck, whose body oozes beyond its undersized shell. (The geoduck, which can burrow three or four feet deep into the tidal flats of Puget Sound, can weigh as much as ten pounds.)

Your eyes will be challenged by an apparently endless combination of powerful surf and rocky headlands, where one early explorer, Juan Rodríguez Cabrillo, noted while sailing along the Big Sur coastline in 1542 that "it seemed as if the mountains would fall upon the ships." Though the coastal ranges seem immutable, they have been stretched, compressed, faulted, folded, and drowned on a virtual geologic torture rack of glaciers and earthquakes.

Millions of years ago, shell deposits collected on the ocean floor. Today that seabed, long ago pushed up and carved by glaciers, is Washington's Olympic Mountains, a range towering 8,000 feet over the Pacific. The Channel Islands off the coast of southern California are the peaks of a range once linked to the mainland.

The coastal ranges still move, sometimes with the jolt of an earthquake that can tumble you out of bed. In another geologic process, in the Palos Verdes Hills of southern California, heavy rains sometimes turn the unconsolidated soils of ancient beach terraces into rock-strewn, tree-snapping landslides.

To a visitor accustomed to clearly defined skies and horizons, this shore can be a letdown; its rugged countenance emerges from and recedes into haze, fog, and overcast. But the shifting, sometimes illusive light imparts a special quality, transforming coastal slopes into undulating, purple humps that seem ready to float into the sky or deflate at the touch of a fallen pine needle. On a San Francisco wharf or an Oregon headland you can watch afternoon fogs roll in and shroud bridges and bluffs. Soon your skin feels a damp touch, and your vision softens into mist, for as Robert Louis Stevenson once wrote, "The sea, in its lighter order, has submerged the earth."

One day my son and I were exploring the Oregon dunes when fog enveloped us. I could hear my son's voice, but I couldn't see him; I couldn't even see my own footprints. My vision wasn't good enough to avoid sandblasted tree trunks or a dune-impounded lake, so I stopped in my tracks. When the fog began to lift as quickly as it had moved in, my son reappeared smiling at me. We shouted greetings and resumed our journey through drifting dunes and stands of trees being slowly buried by sand.

In the lush rain forests of Washington's Olympic National Park, shafts of light leak through the forest canopy; the next century's firs and spruces emerge as sprigs from the moldering trunks of fallen giants. The warmth of decay helps the seedlings grow while their roots stretch down into the damp earth.

Flood waters carry some fallen limbs out of the forest and onto the shore, where they are abraded by sand, polished by surf, and bleached silver-gray by the sun. Children of the summer beach use the wood to make forts, lookouts, even the shapes of dinosaurs. In the fall, when they return to school, their creations topple in the storm surf.

While the Olympic Mountains average more than 100 inches of rain each year, the coastal ranges of central and southern California get by with about 10. By fall the dry coastal slopes, without a raindrop for eight months, look as if they have popped out of an immense toaster. Searing winds sweep in from the desert and suck up any remaining moisture, turning canyon creeks into dusty jokes. Then the huge offshore dome of high-pressure air that has diverted storms away from the land begins to retreat south.

The first teasing rains of November dry quickly on the parched ground. But one night the drops persist; soon ropes of water flow from my eaves. Runoff in street gutters becomes strong enough to float fallen leaves and deep enough to soak the shoes of children exulting in the winter rains. After the storm, stiff sea winds polish washed-out skies to a blue brilliance. A hike up a nearby hill rewards me with views of familiar geology revealed once again in bright winter light.

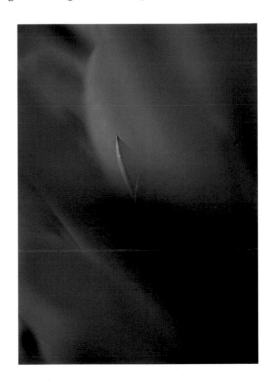

By December creeks resume their swift runs to the Pacific. I clamber up a rain-slicked canyon to see waterfalls and churning white rapids reborn. Cobbles once covered with dust gleam like gems under winter freshets. Canyon creeks converge on sand bottomed rivers that traverse the coastal plain, sending plumes of sediment into the surf. This cargo is the land's gift to the coast; much of the sediment is composed of sand grains that help form and sustain the veneer of beaches covering the wave-cut terraces of the shore.

The rains that revive rivers and beaches also transform the slopes near my Orange County home in southern California. The San Joaquin Hills shine emerald green, sea breezes ruffle through silky meadows, and deer and cattle graze on steep pastures brightened with red paint-brush and blue lupines.

Our coastal wildflowers are small by most standards. They would be lost in the shade of a fat, cultivated rose. But these tiny flowers gain strength in numbers: blankets of field mustard change green hills to yellow, patches of bluebells turn slopes into blue cascades, and purple straw-flowers transform highway shoulders into ribbons of color.

Frost, of course, could end this botanical show, but killing chills are rare. That great heat sink, the Pacific Ocean, keeps temperatures moderate throughout much of the year. Extremes of wet and dry link the soft winter rains, the New Year flowering of the gooseberry, ephemeral rivers, and sandy beaches. It is very much a land of change, even without white winters.

Water birds are partial to the winter greening. Each year thousands of pintails descend upon coastal bays and marshes, while blue herons stalk the shallows of coastal

lagoons, impaling passing fish with their beaks. In deserted lots brightened by sunflowers, white forms of foraging egrets snap open in flight. The V-shaped formations of Canada geese fly overhead on their way to the next green meadow, their passage a welcome interruption to my winter gardening.

While much of the shore along southern California is lined with sandy beaches, the coast from Point Conception to Vancouver is more rocky. Waves slam into cliffs, exerting as much as 1,200 pounds of pressure per square inch, sculpting bedrock into sea caves and spires. From afar these shores seem lifeless; only when you are astride the tide pools do the rich colors of life begin to emerge — the orange of starfish, the shiny black of mussels, the pink of coralline algae, the bronze of palm kelp, the purple of sea urchins. Nourished by tides rich in plankton, this wave-resistant life competes for space.

Life piles on life: algae atop barnacles, barnacles atop mussels, mussels atop more mussels. The mussel beds, encumbered with growth, become top-heavy and vulner-able to the crashing surf. The sea anemone that waits below the mussel bed can expect, sooner or later, a bounty of fallen life within reach of its stinging tentacles. The finfish of these tide pools can evade the shock of waves by wedging themselves into rock crevices. To outwit bigger predators that may come with high tides, tidal fish become masters of camouflage, shifting their pigments from tan to green to red to match their surroundings and confuse their pursuers.

While little fish perform their dazzling color changes, a two-ton elephant seal may sleep on the beach of an offshore island. When I saw my first elephant seal, I thought I was viewing the epitome of sloth. The huge form seemed anchored by its own girth.

Scientists at the Institute for Marine Sciences at the University of California at Santa Cruz have made some remarkable observations of these creatures. Wary of competition from younger rivals, bulls guard their harems of 15 or more females, never leaving the rookery to feed during a breeding season that can last as long as 3 months. They take only catnaps between copulations. After the females return to sea, the bulls, now one-third their former weight, rest for a few days before following them to feed.

Once in the water, the seemingly awkward animal becomes a formidable hunter, chasing down skates, sharks, and other marine animals. The elephant seal handles the desperate maneuvers of its prey with the aplomb of a jet pilot tailing prop planes. Elephant seals can dive 2,000 feet and stay submerged for as long as 48 minutes. Today, when I see an elephant seal lounging on a sand spit or coming up for air in a kelp bed, I no longer see sloth; I see a kind of evolutionary genius superbly adapted to commute between the convoluted terrain of the shore and the rich food pastures of the ocean.

As a young boy eager to catch the next wave, I took this shore for granted as an outdoor stage for my pleasure and excitement. As an adult, I find this dynamic coast a continuous source of wonder and concern. I return to a boyhood beach and find a graffiti-covered sea wall instead of sand. Dams and harbor jetties impound the sand that once nourished a familiar shore. Smog generated by millions of auto exhausts snuffs out the natural, shifting light. High-rises pinch off vistas and sunsets; in some places parking lots are the only horizons. Coastal villages where artists and middle-class families could once afford to live have evolved into boutique ghettos where dozens of merchants offer T-shirts silk-screened with double entendres, but there's no one to repair a shoe, a surfboard, or a small boat.

The more high-rises and No Trespassing signs I see, the more I appreciate the foresight of people who, long before the advent of Earth Day and environmental impact statements, worked to protect the natural shore that my family and I enjoy today. I can hike along a sandstone ridge that was once seabed because more than 70 years ago a woman named Ellen Scripps acquired this scenic site as a reserve rather than see it subdivided. Torrey

Pines State Reserve is a premier place to rediscover the Pacific shore as the first explorers saw it.

During the 1950s, the federal government decided to auction off a small island north of Santa Cruz that was no longer needed as a lighthouse site. The island was offered

to California for park use for $18,000, but the state legislature procrastinated. The highest bidder turned out to be a restaurant owner ready to convert this "raw land" into a resort by building a causeway to the mainland and evicting the residents, a teeming rookery of sea lions. When news of the development plan flashed across TV screens in nearby San Francisco, state legislators were deluged with protests that the Pacific shore needed fewer resorts and more islands. The state acquired the island at the last minute.

If I want to catch another glimpse of the vitality and natural spirit of the Pacific shore, I can view Año Nuevo Island from the mainland and hear, like the roar from a distant stadium, the sound of reprieved sea lions barking into the winds. This eight-acre island sustains a rookery of 12,000 sea lions and 3,000 sea elephants. I don't feel like a stranger when I visit this section of shore; I am more at home with islands I can't reach than with resorts that are too conveniently, oppressively accessible.

Even when you throw that first surf-polished pebble, the Pacific shore has a way of burrowing into your spirit and shaping your perceptions. Many people along the shore are no longer willing to settle for protecting the last vestiges of wilderness. They are bent on reclaiming and expanding this wild domain.

In San Francisco Bay and Upper Newport Bay in southern California, old salt dikes have been torn down so that tides can reclaim mud flats and shore birds can return to feeding grounds. In Puget Sound, Volunteers for Outdoor Washington restore saltwater marshes that once fringed the shore, and scuba divers have removed derelict fishing nets that snared passing crabs, herrings, and seals.

Sewage that once polluted clam beds in California's Humboldt Bay is now treated and used by the community of Arcata to restore freshwater wetlands. In Bellevue, Washington, streams once clogged with silt and logs are being cleaned up so that salmon can return to spawn alongside urban office buildings. In Redwood National Park, more than 200 miles of old logging roads that once blocked streams with silt are being planted with red alder, Douglas fir, and redwood seedlings.

Reversing the rush towards coastal development has its rewards. This, after all, is the Pacific shore at its best, open to the tides, the shifting light, and to children with nothing better to do than make a dinosaur of driftwood, a shore that is unwalled, unsigned, unmitigated, and ungated, wild to the core, a life-giving medium for rock-bound mussels and deep-diving seals, a life-restoring medium for us.

*Wesley Marx*
*Irvine, California*

10

BARKLEY SOUND, BRITISH COLUMBIA

STARFISH AND KELP, BARKLEY SOUND, BRITISH COLUMBIA

TWO ENTWINED STARFISH, TATOOSH ISLAND, WASHINGTON

Doc was collecting marine animals in the Great Tide Pool on the tip of the Peninsula. It is a fabulous place: when the tide is in, a wave-churned basin, creamy with foam, whipped by the combers that roll in from the whistling buoy on the reef. But when the tide goes out the little water world becomes quiet and lovely. The sea is very clear and the bottom becomes fantastic with hurrying, fighting, feeding, breeding animals. Crabs rush from frond to frond of the waving algae. Starfish squat over mussels and limpets, attach their million little suckers and then slowly lift with incredible power until the prey is broken from the rock. And then the starfish stomach comes out and envelops its food. Orange and speckled and fluted nudibranchs slide gracefully over the rocks, their skirts waving like the dresses of Spanish dancers. And black eels poke their heads out of crevices and wait for prey. The snapping shrimps with their trigger claws pop loudly. The lovely colored world is glassed over. Hermit crabs like frantic children scamper on the bottom sand. And now one, finding an empty snail shell he likes better than his own, creeps out, exposing his soft body to the enemy for a moment, and then pops into the new shell. A wave breaks over the barrier, and churns the glassy water for a moment and mixes bubbles into the pool, and then it clears and is tranquil and lovely and murderous again.

John Steinbeck  CANNERY ROW

(LEFT) GULLS, TATOOSH ISLAND, WASHINGTON

STELLER SEA LION, BARKLEY SOUND, BRITISH COLUMBIA

GRAY WHALE, BARKLEY SOUND, BRITISH COLUMBIA

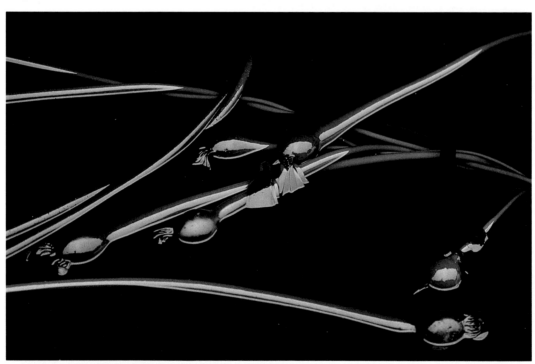

BULL KELP IN TIDE POOL, TATOOSH ISLAND, WASHINGTON

(RIGHT) SEA GULLS, TATOOSH ISLAND, WASHINGTON

LIGHTHOUSE AT DUSK, TATOOSH ISLAND, WASHINGTON

CORMORANT, TATOOSH ISLAND, WASHINGTON

SAILBOAT, BARKLEY SOUND, BRITISH COLUMBIA

(RIGHT) ROCKS AND SEA GRASS, VANCOUVER ISLAND, BRITISH COLUMBIA

BLACK BEAR, VANCOUVER ISLAND, BRITISH COLUMBIA

OCEAN INLET, VANCOUVER ISLAND, BRITISH COLUMBIA

## Evening Ebb

The ocean has not been so quiet for a long while; five night-
    herons
Fly shorelong voiceless in the hush of the air
Over the calm of an ebb that almost mirrors their wings.
The sun has gone down, and the water has gone down
From the weed-clad rock, but the distant cloud-wall rises. The
    ebb whispers.
Great cloud-shadows float in the opal water.
Through rifts in the screen of the world pale gold gleams, and the
    evening
Star suddenly glides like a flying torch.
As if we had not been meant to see her; rehearsing behind
The screen of the world for another audience.

Robinson Jeffers

SEA STACKS AT DUSK, SHI SHI BEACH, WASHINGTON

SEA URCHINS, TATOOSH ISLAND, WASHINGTON

SEA ANEMONES AND STARFISH, SHI SHI BEACH, WASHINGTON

(LEFT AND ABOVE) MOSS-COVERED TREES IN HOH RAIN FOREST,
OLYMPIC NATIONAL PARK, WASHINGTON

(LEFT) AERIAL, LOW TIDE IN GRAYS HARBOR, WASHINGTON

SANDPIPERS OVER GRAYS HARBOR, WASHINGTON

DETAIL OF TUGBOAT, SAN FRANCISCO, CALIFORNIA

CARGO SHIP, ASTORIA, OREGON

CAPE KIWANDA STATE PARK, OREGON

BLEACHED LOGS NEAR CAPE MEARES STATE PARK, OREGON

SAND DUNES AND BEACH GRASS,
OREGON DUNES NATIONAL RECREATION AREA, OREGON

DEAD TREES ENGULFED BY SAND,
OREGON DUNES NATIONAL RECREATION AREA, OREGON

I finally emerged at the base of a steep bank of golden sand and clambered upward on all fours, filling pockets and shoes. The Oregon dunes are of the finest, cleanest, and most uniform sand found in America; constantly moving, forever sifted by summer winds and washed by winter rains, and extending in some areas for miles without tree or bush or flower, too orderly to be the work of haphazard nature and too immense to be the product of man, they present an unreal world to even the casual observer—to my already cockeyed eye, as I achieved the crest of the bank, the dunes presented a terrain forbidding in the extreme.

Ken Kesey  SOMETIMES A GREAT NOTION

OREGON DUNES NATIONAL RECREATION AREA, OREGON

LOG ON EOCENE SANDSTONE, CAPE ARAGO STATE PARK, OREGON

SANDSTONE, CAPE ARAGO STATE PARK, OREGON

PORT ORFORD, OREGON

FISHING BOATS ON DOCK, PORT ORFORD, OREGON

NEAR GOLD BEACH, OREGON

GOATS, BOARDMAN STATE PARK, OREGON

BOARDMAN STATE PARK, OREGON

BEACH GRASS, GOLD BEACH, OREGON

WEATHERED LOGS, CAPE BLANCO STATE PARK, OREGON

PISTOL RIVER STATE PARK, OREGON

REDWOOD NATIONAL PARK, CALIFORNIA

It's not only their unbelievable stature, nor the color which seems to shift and vary under your eyes, no, they are not like any trees we know, they are ambassadors from another time. They have the mystery of ferns that disappeared a million years ago into the coal of the carboniferous era. They carry their own light and shade. The vainest, most slap-happy and irreverent of men, in the presence of redwoods, goes under a spell of wonder and respect. Respect—that's the word. One feels the need to bow to unquestioned sovereigns. I have known these great ones since my earliest childhood, have lived among them, camped and slept against their warm monster bodies, and no amount of association has bred contempt in me. And the feeling is not limited to me.

John Steinbeck  TRAVELS WITH CHARLEY

FERN CANYON, PRAIRIE CREEK REDWOODS STATE PARK, CALIFORNIA

ROOSEVELT ELK,
PRAIRIE CREEK REDWOODS STATE PARK, CALIFORNIA

HOUSE NEAR BEACH, MENDOCINO, CALIFORNIA

OLD GABLES, MENDOCINO, CALIFORNIA

SEA PALMS IN SURF, SHELTER COVE, CALIFORNIA

SHELTER COVE, CALIFORNIA

PALEOCENE SANDSTONE, SALT POINT STATE PARK, CALIFORNIA

SEA FIGS AND BEACH GRASS, NEAR BODEGA BAY, CALIFORNIA

DAIRY CATTLE GRAZING NEAR TOMALES BAY, CALIFORNIA

(RIGHT) FALLOW DEER, POINT REYES NATIONAL SEASHORE, CALIFORNIA

## Gray Weather

It is true that, older than man and ages to outlast him, the Pacific
    surf
Still cheerfully pounds the worn granite drum;
But there's no storm; and the birds are still, no song; no kind of
        excess;
Nothing that shines, nothing is dark;
There is neither joy nor grief nor a person, the sun's tooth
sheathed in cloud,
And life has no more desires than a stone.
The stormy conditions of time and change are all abrogated, the
        essential
Violences of survival, pleasure,
Love, wrath and pain, and the curious desire of knowing, all
perfectly suspended.
In the cloudy light, in the timeless quietness,
One explores deeper than the nerves or heart of nature, the womb
        or soul,
To the bone, the careless white bone, the excellence.

Robinson Jeffers

LIMANTOUR BEACH, POINT REYES NATIONAL SEASHORE, CALIFORNIA

PELICANS, CHANNEL ISLANDS NATIONAL PARK, CALIFORNIA

(RIGHT) SLEEPING BULL ELEPHANT SEAL, AÑO NUEVO STATE RESERVE, CALIFORNIA

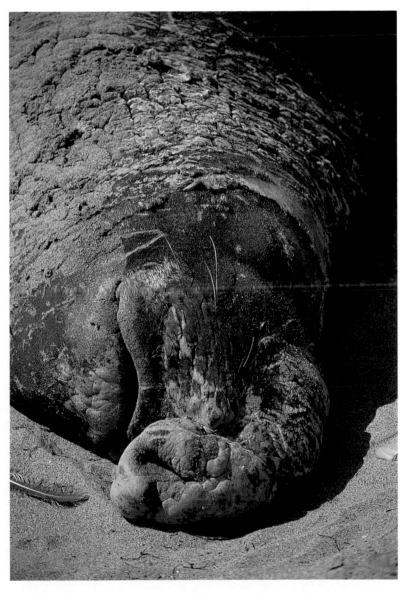

ELEPHANT SEAL IN KELP,
FARALLON NATIONAL WILDLIFE REFUGE, CALIFORNIA

ELEPHANT SEAL,
AÑO NUEVO STATE RESERVE, CALIFORNIA

PIER, FISHERMAN'S WHARF, MONTEREY, CALIFORNIA

CALIFORNIA SEA LION, MONTEREY, CALIFORNIA

SCULPTED SANDSTONE, POINT LOBOS STATE RESERVE, CALIFORNIA

STARFISH AND KELP, POINT LOBOS STATE RESERVE, CALIFORNIA

PINNACLE COVE, POINT LOBOS STATE RESERVE, CALIFORNIA

SEA FIGS, CARMEL, CALIFORNIA

KELP ON SANDSTONE AND SILTSTONE BEACH,
POINT LOBOS STATE RESERVE, CALIFORNIA

SAND PATTERNS,
TORREY PINES STATE RESERVE, CALIFORNIA

(LEFT) WINTERING MONARCH BUTTERFLIES ON BEARD LICHEN,
POINT LOBOS STATE RESERVE, CALIFORNIA

MONTEREY CYPRESSES, POINT LOBOS STATE RESERVE, CALIFORNIA

ROUTE ONE ALONG THE COAST, BIG SUR, CALIFORNIA

WAVES RUSHING THROUGH ROCK TUNNEL,
JULIA PFEIFFER BURNS STATE PARK, BIG SUR, CALIFORNIA

AERIAL OF HILLS, BIG SUR, CALIFORNIA

Pines grew here along the cliff, outlining with tawny stem and dark magnificence of foliage the most exquisite of vistas. The coast was broken by little bays full of brown seaweed that rose and fell indolently with the slow breathing of the sea. Islets were scattered along as if they had been dropped like pebbles out of a full hand. I do not think there can be anywhere on our shores a more enchanting piece of coast than this and the next ten miles to the north. It is the acme of what is generally named the romantic in sea scenery, and is calculated, I should think, to throw an artist into a frenzy in which he would paint one final and conscious masterpiece, then close color-box, camp-stool, and umbrella, and hurl them all over the cliff together.

J. Smeaton Chase CALIFORNIA COAST TRAILS

FISHING BOATS, MORRO BAY, CALIFORNIA

REFLECTION OFFSHORE, SANTA BARBARA, CALIFORNIA

(LEFT AND ABOVE) ANACAPA ISLANDS,
CHANNEL ISLANDS NATIONAL PARK, CALIFORNIA

ELEPHANT SEALS,
CHANNEL ISLANDS NATIONAL PARK, CALIFORNIA

CALIFORNIA SEA LIONS,
POINT BENNETT, CHANNEL ISLANDS NATIONAL PARK, CALIFORNIA

SEASHELLS AND ROCK, PALOS VERDES, CALIFORNIA

(RIGHT) ERODED SANDSTONE CLIFFS,
TORREY PINES STATE RESERVE, CALIFORNIA

SEA GULL AND CLIFFS, TORREY PINES STATE RESERVE, CALIFORNIA

(RIGHT) PELICANS, AÑO NUEVO STATE RESERVE, CALIFORNIA

Pelicans

Four pelicans went over the house,
Sculled their worn oars over the courtyard: I saw
        that ungainliness
Magnifies the idea of strength.
A lifting gale of sea-gulls followed them; slim yachts
        of the element,
Natural growths of the sky, no wonder
Light wings to leave sea; but those grave weights toil,
        and are powerful,
And the wings torn with old storms remember
The cone that the oldest redwood dropped from, the tilting
        of continents,
The dinosaur's day, the lift of new sea-lines.
The omnisecular spirit keeps the old with the new also.
Nothing at all has suffered erasure.
There is life not of our time. He calls ungainly bodies
As beautiful as the grace of horses.
He is weary of nothing; he watches air-planes; he watches
        pelicans.

Robinson Jeffers

SANDSTONE AND SILTSTONE CLIFFS,
TORREY PINES STATE RESERVE, CALIFORNIA

SEASHELL AND THINLY BEDDED SANDSTONE,
ABALONE COVE BEACH, PALOS VERDES, CALIFORNIA

(ABOVE AND RIGHT) NEAR CABO SAN LUCAS, BAJA CALIFORNIA

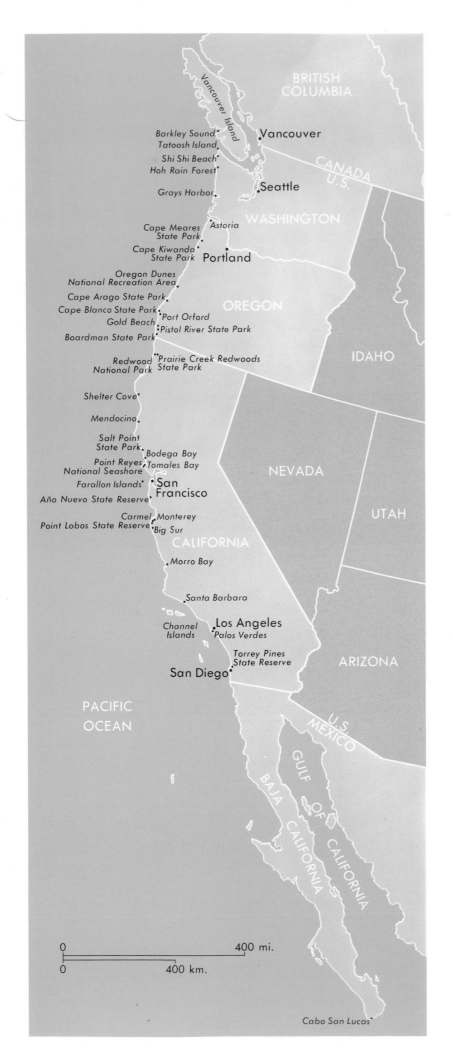

PHOTOGRAPHS TAKEN IN OR NEAR THESE LOCATIONS
CAN BE FOUND ON THE FOLLOWING PAGES:

BRITISH COLUMBIA

Vancouver Island: 23, 24, 25

Barkley Sound: 10-11, 12, 15, 16-17, 22-23,

WASHINGTON

Tatoosh Island: 9, 13, 14, 18, 19, 20, 21, 28

Shi Shi Beach: 27, 29

Hoh Rain Forest: 30, 30-31

Grays Harbor: 32, 33

OREGON

Astoria: 35

Cape Meares State Park: 37

Cape Kiwanda State Park: 36

Oregon Dunes National Recreation Area: 38, 39, 40-41

Cape Arago State Park: 42, 43

Cape Blanco State Park: 50

Port Orford: 44-45, 45

Gold Beach: 4, 46-47, 49

Pistol River State Park: 51

Boardman State Park: 47, 48, 52-53

CALIFORNIA

Redwood National Park: 54

Prairie Creek Redwoods State Park: 56, 57

Shelter Cove: 60, 60-61

Mendocino: 58, 59

Salt Point State Park: 62

Bodega Bay: 7, 63

Tomales Bay: 64

Point Reyes National Seashore: 8, 65, 67

San Francisco: 34

Farallon Islands: 70

Año Nuevo State Reserve: 69, 71, 99

Monterey: 72-73, 73

Carmel: 77

Point Lobos State Reserve: 74, 75, 76, 78, 80, 80-81

Big Sur: 2-3, 82, 83, 84, 86-87

Morro Bay: 88

Santa Barbara: 89

Channel Islands: 1, 68-69, 90, 91, 92, 93, 94-95

Palos Verdes: 96, 101

Torrey Pines State Reserve: 79, 97, 98-99, 100

BAJA CALIFORNIA

Cabo San Lucas: 102, 103